What Others Are Saying

"Pastor Castano was a member of the founding team that formed *Houston Area Pastor Council* in 2003 and has been one of our most committed and dedicated pastoral leaders in the city of Houston. He continues to stand in unity with pastors and bring biblical truth to the arenas of culture and government.

His first hand perspective on the epic and heroic stand against, and the defeat of Mayor Annise Parker's 'Houston Equal Rights Ordinance' provides outstanding insight for other pastors about the *why* and the *how* of unity in Christ and godly citizenship!"
--Rev. Dave Welch, Founder and Executive Director, *Houston Area Pastor Council*

"With incredible detail and a focus on God's Word, Pastor Hernan Castano shares very personal and important insight about his life; and the inspiration that led him to take a stand for religious freedom that was seen around the world. As a fellow Hispanic and Christian who was born and raised in Houston, I could not be more proud to stand with Pastor Castano in support of this book and his continued incredible work for truth and justice." --Jonathan Saenz, President of Texas Values.

"This book is an excellent read from the spirit and heart of Pastor Castano. Thank you, my friend, for sharing this view from your participation in what was a crucial time in the City of Houston." --Pastor Willie Ray Davis

PERSECUTED

Government's Assault on The Church

Hernan Castano

© Copyright 2016 by Hernan Castano

All rights reserved. No part of this publication may be reproduced or transmitted in any form or by any means electronic or mechanical, including photocopying and recording, or by any information storage and retrieval system, except in the case of brief quotations for use in articles and reviews, without written permission from the author.

The views expressed in this book are the author's and do not necessarily reflect those of the publisher.

Pastor Hernan Castano
12500 Corona Lane
Houston, TX 77072
281-564-6247

7710-T Cherry Park Dr, Ste 224
Houston, Texas 77095
http://WorldwidePublishingGroup.com
(713) 766-4271

Paperback: 978-1-68411-189-3

Contents

Acknowledgements 7

Introduction 13

Chapter 1: The Government Subpoenas Pastors in America 29

Chapter 2: The Deception of Equal Rights 45

Chapter 3: Love Is Not Hate 63

Chapter 4: Stand 77

Chapter 5: In Conclusion 89

Appendix A 95

Appendix B - Pictures 97

Acknowledgements

Why I Am Writing This Book?

This book is not written because of my desire to be a writer, or any great ability that I may have to articulate my deep love for God and his commandments. In fact, I am the least of all the great men and women that I stood next to during the battle in Houston, a battle that brought persecution against us the pastors for preaching on the issues of morality and family according to the Bible.

I am simply a Hispanic pastor, an ordained minister called to preach the gospel of Jesus Christ, who was teaching a Bible class on a regular Wednesday night when through the doors of the church a city worker came with the subpoena papers. The subpoena documents were demanding my sermons, and they were sent by the Mayor of the City of Houston, Annise Parker, through her attorneys.

This is why I feel the urgency to write this book even though I have never written any book in English, as my congregation is mainly Hispanic and all my published books are in Spanish. I find myself with an obligation to share the story of how we in Houston experienced the attack against our religious liberty, granted to us by the Constitution of the United States; and how the abusive power in government is trying to intimidate and silence the voice of the church in America.

As the first Latino pastor to have ever been served a subpoena demanding my sermons and a list of other documents, I write this book to let those who want to intimidate the pastors of America know, that we will not hide anymore within the walls of our church buildings. We will not be silenced by the trespassing of government on church property with the intent to manipulate religion. I write this book to sound the alarm, to awaken the church and to call upon those who still believe in what the founding fathers of this nation believed, that we are one nation under God, a nation of the people, for the people and by the people.

However, this book is not about me. Its purpose is to honor God and to acknowledge some of the great spiritual leaders in our nation, the home of the brave and land of the free. One of those men is Pastor Dave Welch, Director of our *Texas Pastor Council*, who has been able to form a strong coalition of American spiritual leaders that includes all minorities and ethnic groups. Pastor Dave is a general in the church and is one of the Houston five who received the subpoena as well.

Another friend and pastor who has my utmost respect, whose voice for justice is an inspiration to many is Houston Pastor Steve Riggle. His wisdom and leadership is a gift to the body of Christ. I want to also recognize other men and women of God who were instrumental in the frontlines of this battle including: Rev. F.N. Williams, Rev. Max Miller, Pastor Willie Davis, Pastor Khanh Huynh, Magda Hermida, and the pastors, leaders, and Christians from across the nation who prayed for us, sent Bibles to Houston's City Hall, and even came to Houston to support us.

I'm also grateful to Senator Ted Cruz, who, after hearing about the subpoenas against the pastors, immediately came and stood beside us, and raised his voice to protect our religious freedom. I wish to thank Governor Mike Huckabee, who called upon the church and all Americans to reject this type of governmental action we experienced in Houston.

We were blessed to have Texas Governor Greg Abbott, who promptly sent a letter to our Mayor to demand that such a violation of our civil rights and religious freedom be stopped. Let us not forget my friend, Attorney Andy

Taylor, who represented us in court against fourteen attorneys working for the Mayor as Goliath to stop the people from voting on the ordinance. Andy was filled with divine grace, wisdom and truth to stand strong as he did those long days at the courthouse. Will never forget when Andy placed those five books, filled with signatures of the people of Houston, in front of the jury and asked that they restore the people's right to vote. That God-given victory was later achieved by a nine to zero Supreme Court Decision in our favor on Friday, July 24, 2015.

We are grateful for the *Alliance Defending Freedom* attorneys who defended us during the subpoenas, until the Mayor withdrew them under pressure. Another great help was the support of Texas Values under the leadership of its president, my friend Attorney Jonathan Saenz. From Washington D.C. we had the support of the *Family Research Council* under the leadership of Tony Perkins, who organized the *I Stand* Sunday in Houston, a gathering which brought the eyes of the nation upon Houston.

We thank God for Dr. Ed Young of *Second Baptist Church*, Houston, who spoke courageously on the issues of this ordinance to his church and to our city. As a Latino leader and pastor, I want to also recognize the support of my friend Rev Samuel Rodriguez, president of the *National Hispanic Christian Leadership Conference*.

Most importantly, let me recognize my dear wife, Wendy Castano, who stood by me with her prayerful support during the long months of these attacks when everywhere we went we had to fight for biblical moral values. Together we serve as pastors of *Rios De Aceite Church* (Rivers of Oil Church) in Houston, a Latino community church. We thank God for each of our church's members for never doubting our stand for religious liberty, even though they were also victims of intimidation by government in Houston.

In summary, the people of Houston who voted "NO" to the proposition deserve our gratitude. The battle was won because of all the people who prayed and believed in the victory of justice and truth. It was proven on November 3, 2015 that the voice of the church, the voice of the people and their actions do make a difference.

Thank You.

Introduction

As we look at the spiritual condition of America today, and at the coldness of men's hearts, remember that Jesus spoke of times like these when he said, *"Because of the increase of wickedness, the love of most will grow cold,"* (Mathew 24:12).

Any nation that turns away from God, ignores his commandments, and attacks his Word has fallen from its position of righteousness and becomes a nation without salvation and unable to help its people. It is a nation infected by depravity. *"Moreover, our eyes failed, looking in vain for help; from our towers we watched for a nation that could not save us"* (Lamentations 4:17, NIV).

As a result of the depravity of men, corruption enters all forms of society, including government at all levels, resulting in injustice replacing justice, immorality replacing morality, and foolishness with perversion replacing wisdom. The blemish of their own actions is visible and the abuse of power becomes the very weapon of that government to uphold evil and feed it with the laws of sin.

> *"He is the Rock, His work is perfect; for all His ways are justice, a God of truth and without injustice; Righteous and upright is He. They have corrupted themselves; they are not His children, because of their blemish: a perverse and crooked generation.*
>
> *Do you thus deal with the LORD, O foolish and unwise people? Is He not your Father, who bought you? Has He not made you and established you"* (Deuteronomy 32:4-6)?

As local city and state governments allow attacks against established fundamental truths, based on the Word of God, that our nation's founding fathers believed, we sink deeper into the abyss of unfaithfulness and rebellion against God. As our society turns away from the truth and embraces the deceitful ideologies and personal agendas of those who reject the Creator, the betrayal of the rules of creation begins to happen and men start exchanging the truth of God for a lie.

> *"Therefore God also gave them up to uncleanness, in the lusts of their hearts, to dishonor their bodies among themselves, 25 who exchanged the truth of God for the lie, and*

> *worshiped and served the creature rather than the Creator, who is blessed forever. Amen"* (Romans 1:24-25).

With the intent to promote their sexual immorality, their wickedness, covetousness, and debased minds, they maliciously present the need for new laws to protect their lifestyles. They clothe themselves with the garments of equal rights while stealing the rights of others, and they call it love while hating those who do not accept their ways.

Choosing not to retain the knowledge of God, they invent evil things. They call it equal rights, but in reality, they attack the very consciousness of the individual who believes that physical attributes at birth are ordained of God. They make laws to force people of faith in God and his Word to serve their definitions of marriage in defiance of the Creator and to provide for themselves accommodation in public where they can exhibit their sin and infect society's moral and family values.

> *"And even as they did not like to retain God in their knowledge, God gave them over to a debased mind, to do those things which are not fitting; being filled with all unrighteousness,*

sexual immorality, wickedness, covetousness, maliciousness; full of envy, murder, strife, deceit, evil-mindedness; they are whisperers, backbiters, haters of God, violent, proud, boasters, inventors of evil things, disobedient to parents, undiscerning, untrustworthy, unloving, unforgiving, unmerciful" (Romans 1:28-31).

This is the reality of what the *Houston Area Pastors Council* experienced as it rose against the Mayor of Houston, Annise Parker, and her personal agenda as the first openly lesbian Mayor governing the fourth largest city of the United States of America.

In April of 2014, Mayor Parker proposed to City Council an ordinance known as NDO, Non Discrimination Ordinance, advocating the need to protect sexual orientation, gender identity, and gender expression at the cost of forcing business owners and people of religious belief to act against their own consciences regarding faith and religion. The name seemed appropriate as it argued that discrimination was happening because of gender identity and gender expression.

This ordinance had so many revisions to it, and was rushed through so quickly by the Mayor in her pursuit to get it approved, that many of the City Council members expressed their concerns over it. With the intent to continue passage of this ordinance, the Mayor with city attorney, David Feldman, changed the name to ERO, Equal Rights Ordinance, to have a stronger strategy in passing the ordinance. The Mayor and city attorney planted the need for this ordinance in order to stop discrimination for gender identity or expression, and with the argument that Houston needed to be like other cities who had passed similar laws. They pressed hard to get council to approve it.

This ordinance meant the presence of men in women's bathrooms, shower rooms, and locker rooms, placing women and children at risk of voyeurism, photographing and video recording as well as sexual assault.

Secondly, this was an invitation for a potential criminal prosecution of those, who, because of religious belief, could not provide certain services. As a pastor and servant of God, preaching God's Word to a large Hispanic congregation, I understood clearly that many of the people of faith would have to stand and choose who they would serve. Either they were to obey the

God who they worship and hear his Word, or they would serve a government that was abusing its power to force and violate the freedom of religion.

I prayed deeply for what was happening in our city and then the Spirit of the Lord reminded me his word in 1 Thessalonians 2:4, *"But as we have been approved by God to be entrusted with the gospel, even so we speak, not as pleasing men, but God who tests our hearts."*

"Even so we speak," which is today known as freedom of speech and religious liberty granted by God and reaffirmed by America's Bill of Rights. Our founding fathers, the majority of who believed in God and his Word, were inspired by these biblical values as they wrote the Constitution of the United States.

Congress of the United States of America voted on September 25, 1789 the final version of the first ten Amendments to the Constitution, known as the Bill of Rights. The First Amendment state: "Congress shall make no law respecting the establishment of religion, or prohibiting the free exercise thereof." [1]

Houston pastors from all over the city encouraged their members to attend the meetings at City Hall, and to

---

[1] William J. Federer, America's God and Country:Encyclopedia of Quotations (St.Louis, MO: Amerisearch, 2000), 158.

express concern for this ordinance. They were to let City Council know that Houston had no discrimination issues, and that there were other laws that protected minorities.

Secondly, we proclaimed the fact that one's gender identity and expression is a matter of their choosing, and is in no way equal with issues related the color of one's skin or one's physiological characteristics at birth. The danger of allowing any man who thought of himself as a woman, even if not dressed as one, to enter a women's bathroom was evident, as any sexual predator would then easily have access to satisfy any cravings for sexual assault.

We provided several examples of such incidents, and asked the Mayor to allow the people to decide. The answer was a solid NO and in the City Hall meetings, our pastors were not allowed to speak at the top of the list. They rejected the voices of those who opposed the ordinance while those in favor of the ordinance were given priority to speak first. Crowds of people gathered and raised their voices against the ordinance outside of City Hall. Phone calls were placed to all City Council members and despite all of our efforts, the voice of the people of Houston was ignored.

A vote was taken by City Council and the results were nothing more than a sign of what happens when leaders elected by the people ignore the voice of the city they represent. The result was 11 to 6 plus the Mayor's vote who even twitted that this was all about her life.

(Council members who voted FOR the ordinance were: C.O. Bradford, Ellen Cohen, Stephen Costello, Robert Gallegos, Richard Nguyen, Ed Gonzalez, David Robinson, Larry Green, Jerry Davis, and Mike Laster.)

(Council members who voted AGAINST the ordinance were: Dwight Boykins, Jack Christie, Michael Kubosh, Dave Martin, Oliver Pennington, and Brenda Stardig.)

As it will be presented later in this book, a ruler who believes a lie makes of his servants, scoffers of the truth, and sets a city aflame.

> "The righteous considers the cause of the poor, but the wicked does not understand such knowledge. Scoffers set a city aflame, but wise men turn away wrath. If a wise man contends with a foolish man, whether the fool rages or laughs, there is no peace. The bloodthirsty hate the blameless, but the upright seek his well-being. A fool vents all his feelings, but a wise man holds them back. If a ruler pays attention

to lies, all his servants become wicked" (Proverbs 29:7-12).

A city in flames is what Houston became as a result of a government that made the personal agenda of its Mayor, based on her lifestyle, a law that discriminated against religion. The "equal rights ordinance" resulted in no equality at all. The *Houston Area Pastor Council* in unity with many denominations, organizations, large and small churches decided to boldly, but lovingly, resist this evil in the city, and we began to pursue a referendum to overturn "the unequal rights ordinance" as we called it, based on its real identity which attacked the faith of the people.

We learned that the people can directly repeal an ordinance passed by the City Council if an adequate number of qualified signatures are received within the deadline of 30 days after it takes effect or is published (after adoption). The City Council must then either repeal the ordinance or place the measure on the next city election ballot for the vote of the people. A simple majority prevails, and if achieved, the ordinance is repealed.

As a result of the hard work of all concerned, a successful referendum petition drive produced over

55,000 signatures. We pre-verified with VUID or certificate numbers over 31,000 signatures, and submitted them on July 3rd. City Secretary Anna Russell certified 17,269 of them as the required minimum number of signatures to force the Referendum provisions of the City's Charter.

City Secretary Anna Russell "checked" 19,177 signatures, and validated 17,826 of them (A 93% success rate), then she discontinued checking since the minimum required signatures had been reached. Her report was dated August 1st. City Attorney David Feldman then intervened. He rejected entire petitions on technical issues such as legibility of the collector's signature, etc. His work left only 15,249 valid signatures; 2,020 under the required minimum.

His presented his report on August 4th. Since the City Attorney has only an advisory role under the City Charter in the validation process, it is clearly evident that Mr. Feldman's intervention became the reason to deprive the citizens of Houston the right to vote on this referendum! As this assault on the right to petition government became the weapon of the Houston Mayor and her 12-14 attorneys against the voice of the people and the attorney who stood for us, Andy Taylor, the

152nd court room of Judge Robert Schaffer became the next battleground.

For an entire month the city attorneys argued on several reasons why the signatures were not valid. The most abusive attack on those signatures was the fact that signatures were illegible and therefore invalid. If a circulator's signature, the person who had gathered the signatures on a page, was discarded then all of the signatures on that page were deemed invalid. If signatures were crossed out by someone, not even the person who placed his signature, they were not valid. The city's prestigious attorneys presented accusations of all kinds against the voice of the people expressed and represented by their signatures.

As the battle for the America's fourth largest city intensified, with the denial of the rights of the people to vote and the constant attacks on those of us who raised our voices in love for truth and justice, the final act of abusive power by city government came. It was the fulfillment of prophecy and a warning that the attack on the Bill of Rights and freedom of religion and speech in America was real and being done on the pastors of the churches and the pulpits of the nation.

The line of separation between church and state had been crossed and the city government, under the leadership of Mayor Annise Parker, had stepped inside the local church to subpoena pastors and demand sermons among other 15 categories of things. I mentioned the fulfillment of prophecy because Jesus had said, *"Remember the word that I said to you, 'A servant is not greater than his master.' If they persecuted Me, they will also persecute you. If they kept My word, they will keep yours also. But all these things they will do to you for My name's sake, because they do not know Him who sent Me. If I had not come and spoken to them, they would have no sin, but now they have no excuse for their sin"* (John 15:20-22).

We the pastors spoke on the issues of the Bible, and they came after us demanding our speeches and sermons as if we were committing a crime by preaching God's Word. I was one of the five pastors they subpoenaed, the first Hispanic pastor in America. They came to my church with the subpoena documents and attacked my freedom of religion and speech. I write this book as a Hispanic-American pastor praying that the church of Jesus Christ will wake up and be not afraid of the days in which we are living. Be not afraid as the Spirit of the lord is upon those who love and obey his commandments.

> *"For God has not given us a spirit of fear, but of power and of love and of a sound mind"* (2 Timothy 1:7).

I write this book, determined to stand and not be silenced or intimidated by governmental finger pointing. I choose to raise my voice for the millions of Hispanics living in this nation that fled the oppression of their human rights by oppressive dictatorships, including the suppression of their religious liberties. I stand for the moral values, family tradition, and God-given human rights that we all embrace so closely. I stand against the abominable lie that marriage should be redefined to be between people of the same sex. I stand against the unbalanced scale of judges who arrogantly strike down the will of the people. I stand against the subpoena of pastors in America and the denial of their freedom of religion and speech. I stand not as a trouble-maker, but as a Hispanic-American Pastor called by God to stand with others to answer to those who disregard the laws of God and follow the Baals of this nation under a Jezebelic leadership.

> *"Then it happened, when Ahab saw Elijah, that Ahab said to him, "Is that you, O troubler of Israel? And he answered, "I have not troubled Israel, but you and your father's house have, in*

> *that you have forsaken the commandments of the* LORD *and have followed the Baals. Now therefore, send and gather all Israel to me on Mount Carmel, the four hundred and fifty prophets of Baal, and the four hundred prophets of Asherah, who eat at Jezebel's table"* (1 Kings 18:17-19).

I stand to sound the alarm and blow the trumpet to a sleeping church in America that must awake from her sleep and take a stand to save a nation that can no longer save itself. It is late and the morning is coming, we must stand before it is too late.

> *"The night is far spent, the day is at hand. Therefore let us cast off the works of darkness, and let us put on the armor of light. Let us walk properly, as in the day, not in revelry and drunkenness, not in lewdness and lust, not in strife and envy. But put on the Lord Jesus Christ, and make no provision for the flesh, to fulfill its lusts"* (Romans 13:12-14).

We must walk properly, make no provision for the flesh and speak truth to those in bondage, sin and confusion. We must not remain silent. Persecution will continue to come against the people with moral values, faith, and love for humanity. They will hate and not understand us, persecuting us as criminals although we really love them and pray for them to come out of their condition. As they persecute you for your faith, and violate your right to freedom of religion while endorsing their own perversions, remember that you are standing for righteousness sake.

> *"Blessed are those who are persecuted for righteousness' sake, for theirs is the kingdom of heaven. Blessed are you when they revile and persecute you, and say all kinds of evil against you falsely for My sake. Rejoice and be exceedingly glad, for great is your reward in heaven, for so they persecuted the prophets who were before you"* (Mathew 5:10-12).

Chapter 1:
The Government Subpoenas Pastors in America

The pastors of America are the voices of restoration to many who are facing deplorable spiritual and moral conditions. They are the voices that heal a nation facing depression and sorrow. They are the voices that bring hope to the human soul, and speak moral values to society. Pastors are the mentors and prayer leaders on behalf of the people and the cities. They work with law enforcement to reduce crime, with doctors by the beds of the sick to bring healing and hope, and they work walking the streets of the cities to build communities and relationships.

The pastors of America are not enemies or criminals, haters or traitors, and they are not politicians. As pastors, we preach God's Word, biblical values that deal with the issues of mankind, society and the nation. We are preachers inspired by the same truths that the founding fathers of this nation believed and practiced. Why would the Mayor of Houston, Annise Parker want to subpoena us for our sermons, speeches, presentations, texts, emails, telephone messages and even our conversations with church members? This is exactly what attorneys representing her and the city did, and she went on television to declare it was fair game to do so.

It was during a Bible class one Wednesday night in October 2014 that, as I walked from my car into the church building to teach, a lady appeared holding in her hands several sheets of paper asking for the pastor. As the senior pastor of Rios de Aceite (Rivers of Oil) Church I greeted her with love and kindness and asked if she was visiting us for Bible study. In the next few seconds, with visible shame and regret she said, "Pastor, I am just doing my job; but I am here to subpoena you for your sermons and need your signature."

As I looked at the paperwork she handed me I had only one thought. It was, "How can government in America step into the house of God and attack pastors for what they preach?" I signed the subpoena papers and responded to the lady with a smile, saying, "Thank you, and God bless you and forgive those who do this".

Immediately I remembered the scripture of how Jesus had said, *"For if they do these things in the green wood, what will be done in the dry"* (Luke 23:31)?

If they arrested and accused the Lord Jesus for speaking truth and love, then what was happening in Houston to pastors was foretold during the his persecution. It was very clear to me that the subpoena was a weapon of intimidation, a strategy to silence the church's voice, and an attempt to prove the power of government over the will of the people.

A subpoena is understood as an order by the court to testify and to turn over the requested documents or face punishment. It is exactly the same as what happened in the Book of Acts when the disciples were threatened to stop preaching about Jesus, where we read: *"But so that it spreads no further among the people, let us severely threaten them that from now on they speak to no man in this name. So they called them and commanded them not to speak at all nor teach in the name of Jesus"* (Acts 4:17-18).

Why the Subpoena?

1. So that we pastors do not spread any further, the truth, among the people that will reveal the true agenda against freedom of religion in America
2. To stop the teaching of God's Word and limit the effectiveness of our sermons regarding moral and biblical values

3. To cause us to be shaken by the fear of punishment enforced by the power of government
4. They were looking for ways to attack our message and portray it as a hateful, discriminatory voice against the LGBT (Lesbian, gay, bi-sexual and transsexual) community. They wanted us to stop saying that gender identity and expression is a choice the individual makes, and not something he or she is born with.
5. The subpoena was a warning to other church leaders that they were not to speak on behalf of the people, and not to petition government.
6. To control religion, control the faith of the people, and force the pastors to support the so-called equal rights agenda
7. The subpoena was a declaration that religion and freedom of speech from the pulpit was never to be practiced without governmental supervision.

When a government like the one Mayor Annise Parker established in Houston, disrespects the house of God and the pastors, the blood shed by our soldiers for America's freedom of religion and speech is ignored. The subpoena served on the pastors in Houston was the proof to the nation that it was destroying the foundations of the righteousness and giving the country to the wicked.

> *"For look! The wicked bend their bow, they make ready their arrow on the string, that they may shoot secretly at the upright in heart. If the foundations are destroyed, what can the righteous do"* (Psalms 11:2-2)?

The question is what can the righteous do? The answer is, the people must return to God and raise the standard of truth and justice. Pastors have to bring back not only the message of love and forgiveness, but the message that God will not accept a lie that deceives the heart of mankind.

> *"Justice is turned back, and righteousness stands afar off; for truth is fallen in the street, and equity cannot enter. So truth fails, and he who departs from evil makes himself a prey"* (Isaiah 59:14-15).

Truth must be preached again, and the lies of sin disguised as equality must be called by its name regardless of the threat of becoming a prey of those who want to make faith equal with sin.

The Power of Prayer

As I found myself with the subpoena paperwork in my hands, I walked toward the altar of the church and laid the papers there before God exactly as Judah's King Hezekiah did.

> *"And Hezekiah received the letter from the hand of the messengers, and read it; and Hezekiah went up to the house of the LORD, and spread it before the LORD. Then Hezekiah prayed before the LORD, and said: 'O LORD God of Israel, the One who dwells between the cherubim, You are God, You alone, of all the kingdoms of the earth. You have made heaven and earth. Incline Your ear, O LORD, and hear; open Your eyes, O LORD, and see; and hear the words of Sennacherib, which he has sent to reproach the living God'"* (2 Kings 19:14-16).

Prayer is a powerful weapon in the midst of persecution and it allows you to put the battle into God's hands. I prayed that night with fervor and a fire of passion, and praised God for allowing me to be a voice representing moral values and religious freedom in this nation. It is only through prayer that the human soul can find peace in the midst of the storm and in an invasion of darkness.

As they were coming to arrest Jesus for the truth he had spoken so many times, we find that he found his greatest strength in prayer at Gethsemane,

> *"Then Jesus came with them to a place called Gethsemane, and said to the disciples, 'Sit here while I go and pray over there.' And He took with Him Peter and the two sons of Zebedee, and He began to be sorrowful and deeply distressed. Then He said to them, 'My soul is exceedingly sorrowful, even to death. Stay here and watch with Me.'*
>
> *He went a little farther and fell on His face, and prayed, saying, 'O My Father, if it is possible, let this cup pass from Me; nevertheless, not as I will, but as You will.'"*
> (Mathew 26:36-39)

Prayer with Action Brings Change

We must understand that the purpose of prayer is not for us to be able to hide or retreat from our actions and cancel the message of truth. It is with the motivation to surrender to the will of God and to be empowered to take action, bring change, and continue to lift up the will of our Father God. Prayer can change the destiny of a nation, the heart of the people in a city, and the will of the leaders of our government. Prayer will release the supernatural of the spirit world into the natural of the world of men.

Prayer was always done during the persecution of the people of faith who acted according to their freedom of religion and convictions from the heart as inspired by their relationship with God. Daniel prayed when he heard of the law of the land that required no man to pray to God, but to only petition the King. It's time for us to pray and to open even more the windows as a witness that we will not be unfaithful to our God and the right to honor him because of the threat of lions.

> *"Now when Daniel knew that the writing was signed, he went home. And in his upper room, with his windows open toward Jerusalem, he knelt down on his knees three times that day, and prayed and gave thanks before his God, as was his custom since early days.*
>
> *Then these men assembled, and found Daniel praying and making supplication before his God. And they went before the king, and spoke concerning the king's decree: 'Have you not signed a decree, that every man who petitions any god or man within thirty days, except you, O king, shall be cast into the den of lions?'*
>
> *The king answered and said, 'The thing is true, according to the law of the Medes and Persians, which does not alter'"* (Daniel 6:10-12).

God closed the mouths of the lions and preserved the life of Daniel as he decided not to abandon his faith and make it equal to idolatry and false worship promoted by the laws of the Medes and Persians. Thirty days without freedom of religion and speech, thirty days of government imposition in the lives of men, and thirty days of persecution to those who did not obey the decree of the king. Daniel not only resisted such an attack, but he also caused the law to be changed.

> *"Then King Darius wrote to all peoples, nations, and languages, that dwell in all the earth: 'Peace be multiplied to you. I make a decree that in every dominion of my kingdom men must tremble and fear before the God of Daniel. For He is the living God, and steadfast forever; His kingdom is the one which shall not be destroyed, and His dominion shall endure to the end. He delivers and rescues, and He works signs and wonders in heaven and on earth, who has delivered Daniel from the power of the lions'"* (Daniel 6:25-27).

A new law was established as the old one that brought persecution of religion and controlled the expressions of faith was revoked. This must be the route of change that pastors must lead to rescue this nation from decrees of government and even the redefinitions of marriage and moral values being issued by courts at all levels as a means to stop the voice of the church in America.

We as pastors must be the Daniels of today who will open the windows of the house of God to proclaim and exhibit our faith and actions in obedience to God's commandments. As men of God living in a generation that has lost the discernment and wisdom needed to separate truth from deception, we must not only raise our voices. We may also be required to endure persecution, and defamation.

> *"For I think that God has displayed us, the apostles, last, as men condemned to death; for we have been made a spectacle to the world, both to angels and to men. We are fools for Christ's sake, but you are wise in Christ! We are weak, but you are strong! You are distinguished, but we are dishonored! To the present hour we both hunger and thirst, and we are poorly clothed, and beaten, and homeless. And we labor, working with our own hands. Being reviled, we bless; being persecuted, we endure; being defamed, we entreat. We have been made as the filth of the world, the off*

scouring of all things until now" (1 Corinthians 4:9-13).

I believe that the subpoena of my sermons at church was with the intention to destroy the integrity of the ministry, to accuse me as well as other pastors of being filthy and evil extremist filled with hate toward the LGBT community. The strategy of local government was to remove the influence of my ministry by affecting my reputation and credibility as a preacher and teacher of God's Word. This is the same strategy that was practiced in the days of Jesus when he became an enemy to the liberal movement, the sinful generation, and the hypocrisy of the rulers. They brought false accusations, false witnesses, and demanded his execution.

The subpoena is much more than a legal document from a court, it is the voice of politics invading the church, silencing the messengers of God, and crucifying the convictions of Christianity. Judges can only agree to such infamy of the subpoena of pastors if they have sold themselves to the arm of a political agenda.

> *"That they may do evil with both hands earnestly, the prince asketh, and the judge asketh for a reward; and the great man, he uttereth his mischievous desire: so they wrap it up"* Micah 7:3).

I will remind every judge that holds the responsibility of interpreting the law in justice, that they will be judged by a higher authority. Political power and the strength of money can only purchase your soul, but it will never destroy the evidence of truth. This is why, although Judge Schaffer decided in favor of the city government and Mayor Annise Parker by rejecting some of the signatures because they were not legible, at the end of the battle the people of Houston voted and we won.

The message of defeating the equal rights ordinance in November 2015 in Houston by an overwhelming 60.97 percent of the voters who voted against it, was that, when pastors, churches, and citizens with moral values and faith unite as one for justice and family then there is no subpoena that can silence the church. Pastors came from all over the nation and stood next to us in Houston. Side by side we marched and filled the churches, called the media and exposed the attack on the American pulpits and its pastors, and above all we cried out louder than ever raising the standard for freedom of religion.

Men of character, in government, with faith, and integrity also rose up to support us. Governor Mike Huckabee asked every pastor and Christian in the nation to send a Bible to City Hall in Houston. Bibles started coming in by the thousands and the people who had served the subpoena for sermons were submerged under an ocean of letters, Bibles, and sermons. The public outcry to withdraw this attack on the pastors of America and their right to religious freedom was loud. Senator Ted Cruz, was one of the first to fly to Houston and meet with the pastors and to declare publicly that the absurd and abusive action that Houston's government had taken against the Houston five was to stop. Senator Cruz (an attorney himself) spoke bravely, demanding the immediate withdrawal of the subpoenas. When Mayor Parker realized that we were not going to let her intimidate us, or force us to surrender to her terrible ordinance, she withdrew the subpoenas...but not the ordinance, which she was determined to pass. In her own words, it was about her own private life and she was not going to let go.

The People Voted and Decided

On November 3rd, 2015 the nation watched as the media reported a clear and huge victory of the people representing family values and religious freedom over Mayor Annise Parker and her group of City Council members who had earlier denied the right of the people to vote. The official results showed a 60.97% said NO to the equal rights ordinance, unequal rights really, and 39.03% in favor of it. Mayor Parker had to admit the defeat of the ordinance which was crushed by the voters of Houston, but she showed her real character by releasing her inner feelings with offensive and abusive words against the pastors of Houston. She declared on public media that we the pastors were evil, demon possessed and haters. Her words are exactly a reflection of what we are hearing today all over the nation against Christians who refuse to obey the laws of men that are contrary to their religion.

This great victory of justice over injustice, truth over deception, and moral decency over immorality was the result of the church of Jesus Christ coming together, and the unity of the pastors and people in support of family values coming together.

For over 18 months Houston became the spiritual battle ground of what every pastor will describe as the warfare of Ephesians, Chapter 6. Houston became the most talked about city as millions of dollars were invested by the LGBT community and others who wanted to silence the church. President Barak Obama raised his voice, but the church's voice was stronger. Democratic candidate for President of the United States, Hillary Clinton, raised her voice, as did many celebrities, executives of big business, but in the end of it all it was the church, and the common and normal citizens who believe in family, religious freedom, and the constitutional right to vote, whose voices were heard and who won!

> *"For Zion's sake will I not hold my peace, and for Jerusalem's sake I will not rest, until the righteousness thereof go forth as brightness, and the salvation thereof as a lamp that burneth"* (Isaiah 62:1).

Chapter 2:
The Deception of Equal Rights

*"A true witness delivereth souls:
But a deceitful witness speaketh lies"*
(Proverbs 14:25).

The presentation of truth will always bring deliverance to the person who hears it, but a lie presented as truth will only imprison the soul that accepts and believes it. When Jesus was arrested and persecuted, the Bible declares that false witnesses appeared to accuse him.

> *"Now the chief priests, and elders, and all the council, sought false witness against Jesus, to put him to death; But found none: yea, though many false witnesses came, yet found they none. At the last came two false witnesses, and said, This fellow said, I am able to destroy the temple of God, and to build it in three days. And the high priest arose, and said unto him, answerest thou nothing? What is it which these witness against thee? But Jesus held his peace. And the high priest answered and said unto him, I adjure thee by the living God, that thou tell us whether thou be the Christ, the Son of God"* (Matthew 26:59-63).

Deception can only survive with the attacks of false testimony given by those who intend to crucify truth. Persecution of truth is the upholding of evil, the promotion of corruption and the establishment of injustice. During our fight as pastors in Houston to stop this persecution of truth, we encountered many people who testified and spoke many lies against those who oppose the equal rights ordinance. They constantly referred to us as extremists, haters, bigots, and falsely accused us as if we were promoting discrimination. Many of us faced media interviews with reporters who were more interested in supporting the liberal agenda and persecuting people of faith than they were in reporting the truth.

The liberal media were always conducting investigative interviews attempting to manipulate the facts of our position, and publishing misleading information favoring the other side. However, we remain grateful to the networks that were professional and nonpartisan in reporting, who accurately and effectively revealed the violation of the citizens' right to vote that Houston's city government, under Annise Parker, was doing.
Many times false witnesses are brought in to destroy the testimony and the identity of those who have not sold or compromised the power of truth and as a consequence leaving it to fall on the streets of the city. The only way equity cannot enter and truth will not stand, is when we the people who believe in religious

liberty and the existence of God as the giver of truth, do nothing to stop the enemy's lies.

> *"In transgressing and lying against the LORD, and departing away from our God, speaking oppression and revolt, conceiving and uttering from the heart words of falsehood. And judgment is turned away backward, and justice standeth afar off: for truth is fallen in the street, and equity cannot enter. Yea, truth faileth; and he that departeth from evil maketh himself a prey: and the LORD saw it, and it displeased him that there was no judgment"* (Isaiah 59:13-5).

What is a False Witness?

A false witness in one who speaks falsehood from his heart while wrongfully judging the intentions, actions and words of the accused. It is a person who speaks words of deceit, using the tongue as a sword of evil while destroying the foundation of truth with the promotion and exaltation of a lie.

> *"He who speaks truth declares righteousness, but a false witness, deceit. There is one who speaks like the piercings of a sword, but the tongue of the wise promotes health. The truthful lip shall be established forever, but a lying*

> *tongue is but for a moment. Deceit is in the heart of those who devise evil, but counselors of peace have joy"* (Proverbs 12:17-20).

A false witness carries a false identity, a hidden motive and emotion which serves as the power source for the words and actions of his life. He or she presents themselves as victims, as the one being discriminated against, offended, and attacked while leading others to ignore the facts and the evidence regarding the situation.

In Jesus' day there were many who repeated well the exact words of Jesus, but did so out of context. One example is when Jesus talked about his body being the temple that would be raised from the dead in three days. They never understood and instead thought he was referring to the temple which took 46 years to build.

> *"Jesus answered and said to them, 'Destroy this temple, and in three days I will raise it up.' Then the Jews said, 'It has taken forty-six years to build this temple, and will You raise it up in three days?' But He was speaking of the temple of His body. Therefore, when He had risen from the dead, His disciples remembered that He had said this to them; and they believed the Scripture and the word which Jesus had said"* (John 2:19-22).

During those long days, as we pastors and others testified before the City Council and the Mayor, trying to help them see the wrong they were doing, numbers of false witnesses came through with all sorts of arguments, stories, and above all, brought in those who presented themselves as ministers of God's Word to testify against us. They would hold up the Bible and talk about Jesus while they distorted scriptures, and misinterpreted biblical morality. They were doing exactly what Jesus declared of the Sadducees where we read: *"Jesus answered and said to them, 'You are mistaken, not knowing the Scriptures nor the power of God'"* (Matthew 22:29).

False witnesses, dressed with clerical collars, even declared wrongly, that Jesus would approve the equality of marriage (support gay "marriage"), the equality of justice with injustice, and that Christ would even be in favor of the equal rights movement. Paul warned the church of this deception,

> *"Do you not know that the unrighteous will not inherit the kingdom of God? Do not be deceived. Neither fornicators, nor idolaters, nor adulterers, nor homosexuals, nor sodomites, nor thieves, nor covetous, nor drunkards, nor revilers, nor extortionists will inherit the kingdom of God. And such were some of you. But you were washed, but you were sanctified,*

> but you were justified in the name of the Lord Jesus and by the Spirit of our God..."

How dare these false ministers speak lies in the name of the Lord Jesus, how shameful of them to carry a Bible and not understand the very words spoken by the Lord. They are deceitful workers, and as we see in scripture, even Satan himself pretends to be an angel of light.

> "... For such are false apostles, deceitful workers, transforming themselves into apostles of Christ. And no wonder! For Satan himself transforms himself into an angel of light. Therefore, it is no great thing if his ministers also transform themselves into ministers of righteousness, whose end will be according to their works" (2 Corinthians 11:13-15).

Why Not Equality?

God created man in his image. *"And God said, Let us make man in our image, after our likeness: and let them have dominion over the fish of the sea, and over the fowl of the air, and over the cattle, and over all the earth, and over every creeping thing that creepeth upon the earth. So God created man in his own image, in the image of God created he him; male and female created he them"* (Genesis 1:26-27).

The image of God was a result of God's glory upon man. God created man a living spirit being like himself, with a soul (mind, will and emotions), living in an immortal body of light. In the Garden of Eden there was a profound and direct relationship between God and man where Adam understood he was a created being, a special and unique creation made of the dust and with the breath of God.

Paul, in the New Testament, speaks of transformation only possible as man sees God's glory upon himself.

> *"But we all, with open face beholding as in a glass the glory of the Lord, are changed into the same image from glory to glory, even as by the Spirit of the Lord"* (2 Corinthians 3:18).

When Adam and Eve listened to the voice of deception and believed the lie of equality ("You shall be as gods."), they sinned and the glory of God was removed from them. Their relationship with the Creator was lost and they died spiritually. Notice the lie of equality introduced by the serpent. *"And the serpent said unto the woman, Ye shall not surely die: For God doth know that in the day ye eat thereof, then your eyes shall be opened, and <u>ye shall be as gods</u>, knowing good and evil"* (Genesis 3:4-5).

The lie of equality was introduced as a tool to deceive and destroy the very purpose and design of God. Equality can only exist if one believes the deception that one can be as God, which was exactly what the devil told Adam and Eve to get them to believe equal rights. The Creator gives rights to men according to their assignments, design and purpose. If you pay close attention to creation you will know that man was made with a distinct gender identity from day one. *"So God created man in his own image, in the image of God created he him; male and female created he them"* (Genesis 1:27).

God created the male body biologically different than the female body. He did not make the male and female bodies equal. Equality wasn't necessary. Had God had made them duplicates, the purpose and assignment of creation would have been impossible.

When the woman was created, Adam did not say, "Here is another me." Instead, he said, "She is flesh of my flesh and bone of my bones."

> *"And the LORD God caused a deep sleep to fall upon Adam, and he slept: and he took one of his ribs, and closed up the flesh instead thereof; And the rib, which the LORD God had taken from man, made he a woman, and brought her unto the man. And Adam said, 'This is now bone of my bones, and flesh of my flesh: she shall be called Woman, because she was taken out of Man.' Therefore shall a man leave his father and his mother, and shall cleave unto his wife: and they shall be one flesh. And they were*

both naked, the man and his wife, and were not ashamed" (Genesis 2:21-25).

Adam identified God's new creation as having flesh and bones like his, though not like him. He sees the physical, biological differences and immediately understands that his helper is not another male like himself. This is why not all things are equal, and equality can destroy the design and the purpose of creation. As a matter of fact, if God wanted Eve to be physically equal to Adam, then the creator would have given Adam the ability to give birth, but to the contrary only the woman was given the right to bear children in her body.

Not all things created can, nor should be equal. Nature shows us that there are differences and that those differences are important for existence. For example, there is a sun and a moon. Can you imagine if the moon was equal to the sun, if the moon served the earth like the sun does, there would be no distinction between day and night?

Every elementary school student learns that two is not equal to three, nor is three equal to four. The sum of five plus three isn't the same as five minus three. This is why there is a liberal movement fueled by the powers of darkness using the minds of unbelievers in government to destroy the foundation of absolute truth and the biblical moral values of God. Those who want to use equal rights must understand that yes, all humans must be treated fairly, with dignity, and full of respect. However, that does not mean that we must accept their notion of equality and reject our freedom of religion and speech to believe, teach and preach that there is a Creator who alone decides the gender identity of each individual at birth.

In May of 2016, the New York Commission on Human Rights published Dr. David Reagan's list of 31 genders that must be recognized in the workplace, in public areas and in housing. According to the September 2016 edition of *Lamp Lighter*, the Commission declared that a refusal to use a person's preferred name or title can be considered "gender-based harassment," and result in a fine up to $250,000 dollars. We are becoming a nation as confused as Adam and Eve were when they accepted the satanic belief that they could eat of the forbidden fruit and be like God—could change their identity. Here is the list of the 31 genders they published. It clearly shows the depravity of men:

1. Bi-gendered
2. Cross-dresser
3. Drag King

4. Drag Queen
5. Femme Queen
6. Female-to-male
7. FTM
8. Gender Bender
9. Genderqueer
10. Male-to-Female
11. MTF
12. Non-Op
13. HURA
14. Pangender
15. Transexual/Transsexual
16. Trans Person
17. Woman
18. Man
19. Butch
20. Two-Spirit
21. Trans
22. Agender
23. Third Sex
24. Gender Fluid
25. Non-binary Transgender
26. Androgyne
27. Gender Gifted
28. Gender Blender
29. Femme

30. Androgynous
31. Person of Transgender Experience

This is exactly what the Bible tells us in Romans, where men changed the glory of God, and rejected their own gender identity. They decided to change it and redefine it using their vain imaginations. Their foolish heart darkened by sin. This perverted gender identity list is proof of the ungodliness and unrighteousness of men who would dishonor their own bodies, according to the desires of the lusts of the heart.

> *"For the wrath of God is revealed from heaven against all ungodliness and unrighteousness of men, who hold the truth in unrighteousness; Because that which may be known of God is manifest in them; for God hath shewed it unto them. For the invisible things of him from the creation of the world are clearly seen, being understood by the things that are made, even his eternal power and Godhead; so that they are without excuse: Because that, when they knew God, they glorified him not as God, neither were thankful; but became vain in their imaginations, and their foolish heart was darkened. Professing themselves to be wise, they became fools, and changed the glory of the*

incorruptible God into an image made like to corruptible man, and to birds, and four-footed beasts, and creeping things. Wherefore God also gave them up to uncleanness through the lusts of their own hearts, to dishonor their own bodies between themselves: Who changed the truth of God into a lie, and worshipped and served the creature more than the Creator, who is blessed forever. Amen" (Romans 1:18-25).

1. They did not glorify God as God. Equality is only acceptable and correct when it submits to the Creator and accepts that he alone has the right to assign identity, purpose, design, and assignment.

2. They allowed the imaginations of their minds to serve as the guiding principles for their decisions and resolutions instead of the foundation of God's Word. They walked away from reality, they created their own foolish rules to live by.

3. They were deceived by the wisdom of this world, which the Bible describes as earthly, sensual and devilish.

"But if ye have bitter envying and strife in your hearts, glory not, and lie not against the truth. This wisdom descendeth not from above, but is <u>earthly</u>, <u>sensual</u>, <u>devilish</u>. For where envying and strife is, there is confusion and every evil work" (James 3:14-15).

4. They changed the image, that image of who they were created to be, and determined themselves to be like the image of animals, corrupted beings who wanted to be equal to others. Instead of one true identity, some have chosen to have multi-identities, to be a male one day and a female the next.

5. They exchanged the truth of God for a lie, and worshipped the creature rather than the God who created them. The prophet Isaiah said of these times, *"Woe unto them that call evil good, and good evil; That put darkness for light, and light for darkness; That put bitter for sweet, and sweet for bitter"* (Isaiah 5:20)!

Why not equality? There can be no equality when there is a difference in the image, a difference in function, a difference in purpose, and a difference we can all understand. *"Her priests have violated my law, and have profaned mine holy things: they have put no difference between the holy and profane, neither have they shewed difference between the unclean and the clean..."* (Ezekiel 22:26)

We have an obligation as responsible leaders, parents, mentors, and children of God not only to know the difference, but to teach it to others. *"And they shall teach my people the difference between the holy and profane, and cause them to discern between the unclean and the clean"* (Ezekiel 44:23).

The people perish because of lack of knowledge. The generation that will inherit the nation from us must be taught the truth. They must be warned of the dangers of not wisely differentiating between things, and trying to make them equal when they are not. God gives us discernment to protect us from misleading and deceptive information. Discernment is God-given spiritual insight into the deeper reality of the spirit world and its influence on the minds and hearts of men. This is why much of the secular teaching that our children receive in school, the books they are given to read, and the influence that they receive is being nurtured by those who want to erase God and faith from their minds. Teaching biblical principles and perspective must be restored, it must become the priority not only of pastors to their congregations, but of Christian parents to their children.

Another reason there are differences, and that not everything is equal, is because there is power in in our differences. There is unity in differences and beauty in them. The beauty of creation is the difference God gave to everything, different colors reflected in God's rainbow is a sign of the covenant between heaven and earth. It was never intended to be used as a symbol of rebellion against the laws of God or as a symbol of equality. (The LGBT community has adopted the rainbow is their symbol of unity.)

> *"I do set my bow in the cloud, and it shall be for a token of a covenant between me and the earth. And it shall come to pass, when I bring a cloud over the earth, that the bow shall be seen in the cloud: And I will remember my covenant, which is between me and you and every living creature of all flesh; and the waters shall no more become a flood to destroy all flesh. And the bow shall be in the cloud; and I will look upon it, that I may remember the everlasting covenant between God and every living*

> *creature of all flesh that is upon the earth. And God said unto Noah, This is the token of the covenant, which I have established between me and all flesh that is upon the earth"* (Genesis 9:13-17).

Men were rebelling against God and promoting equality of morality with immorality, of a man's body with a woman's body, of depravity and doing all manner of abominations. This brought God's judgment and wrath resulting in a devastating flood that completely covered the earth. Then God placed the rainbow in the sky as a memorable sign of his love and mercy upon all flesh.

One must not assume one kind of seed is equal to the other. God himself said that each seed produces according to its kind. This is why man must respect the laws of nature without equating, mutating, or cloning the seed and its kind.

> *"And God said, Let the earth bring forth grass, the herb yielding seed, and the fruit tree yielding fruit after his kind, whose seed is in itself, upon the earth: and it was so. And the earth brought forth grass, and herb yielding*

seed after his kind, and the tree yielding fruit, whose seed was in itself, after his kind: and God saw that it was good" (Genesis 1:11-12).

Chapter 3:
Love Is Not Hate

Many are offended when confronted by the truth. They judge our words and actions as if they are hate crimes, when in reality they are loving, godly warnings for them to turn from their sins. Sin kills. *"The wages of sin is death"* (Romans 3:23). Love brings restoration to a confused mind. Hate, on the other hand, drowns that same mind in the deep waters of captivity and depravity. Love offers a way out, while hate closes all doors to change. Love brings hope and offers a change in lifestyle, while hate condemns the human soul to a lifetime of bondage. Love builds a relationship with bridges of help and support instead of destroying the channels of support as hate does. Love unites but hate divides.

One of the greatest problems we face today is the criminalization of love being judged as hate. When pastors, who are called to preach the good news of salvation, restoration, and regeneration are seen as hateful, then love is misunderstood. This is why Paul said, *"And I will very gladly spend and be spent for you;*

though the more abundantly I love you, the less I be loved" (2 Corinthians 12:15).

Real love requires an investment of oneself and all one may have, although many will love you less and even persecute you with hate. Christianity is not a religion of hate. We do not seek to discriminate or reject anyone. We only wish to help. We offer real solutions to those who are enslaved and caught in the prison of their own actions. We believe in the power of the Holy Spirit, which is the transforming power that delivers captives from bondage. Jesus gave the perfect example of what love is he laid down his life for others, *"This is my commandment, that ye love one another, as I have loved you. Greater love hath no man than this, that a man lay down his life for his friends"* (John 15:12-13).

All the long hours, the extended court days, the price paid to raise a voice on behalf of justice and moral values were done because we pastors care and pray for those who are spiritually blind. We would not be worthy of our calling had we chosen to remain silent when we saw the Mayor and the majority of council members planning an ordinance of persecution of religion against people of faith. We fought in Houston on behalf of the many men and women who have given their lives, shed their blood in the foreign fields of the world to protect the freedom of this great nation and the freedom of religion and speech we are granted by the Constitution. The only love that wins is a love founded on truth and justice. That is the love that brings conviction to the human heart and transforms it. Love wants the best for others. It will warn them of the consequences of their wrong actions. Love requires one to do what must be done, to speak what must be spoken, and to make a difference in people's lives. This is why God sent his Son into the world, so that Jesus may be a light to all men.

> *"For God sent not his Son into the world to condemn the world; but that the world through him might be saved. He that believeth on him is not condemned: but he that believeth not is condemned already, because he hath not believed in the name of the only begotten Son of God. And this is the condemnation, that light is come into the world, and men loved darkness rather than light, because their deeds were evil. For every one that doeth evil hateth the light, neither cometh to the light, lest his deeds should be reproved"* (John 3:17-20).

Notice that hate is directed toward the light, those who love darkness and do evil refuse to come to the light. The problem is that many people have no understanding of the scriptures today and have foolishly believed that love is the admittance of the worldly actions and the works of the flesh as described in the fifth chapter of Galatians. No minister of the gospel, no believer in the Bible, and no true Christian will support an immoral, unethical, ordinance that defies God's principles. No person who understands the structure of the family and the importance of protecting the future of their children will support an ordinance that places men in women's bathrooms. We must understand the following about love:

1. Love is faithful to one master and does not have two masters. You cannot love God and love the world. (1 John 2:15-17; James 4:4)
2. Love is not afraid to speak the truth. (1 John 4:18)
3. Love will cause one to obey God's commandments, as Jesus did. (2 John 1:6)
4. When someone rejects the love of the truth, they will fall into a strong delusion and believe a lie. (2 Thessalonians 2:10-12)

5. Reconciliation is the ministry of love, which is only possible through Christ as we accept that he died for our sins. (Romans 5:8-11)
6. Love does not hate. It does not work ill toward one's neighbor. We do not oppose proposed ordinances, or wrongful unjustified actions, to do evil. We oppose them to protect our neighbor, to be a voice for future generations, and to prevent the fall of moral and faith values. (Romans 13:10)
7. The greatest threat to society comes with the increase of iniquity and sin, because when iniquity abounds, the love of many is waxed cold. (Mathew 24:12)
8. Love brings correction, but hate spares the rod. (Proverbs 13:24).
9. The discipline of parents to their children is the manifestation of love. (Hebrews 12:7-8)
10. To love yourself is to love your neighbor. (Matthew 19:19)

The treatment of Christians by those who see religion and faith as an obstacle to their desires and intentions to bring equality under the umbrella of protecting discrimination, is the very fulfillment of prophecy in our time. In the words of Jesus, *"Then shall they deliver you up to be afflicted, and shall kill you: and ye shall be hated of all nations for my name's sake. And then shall many be offended, and shall betray one another, and shall hate one another"* (Matthew 24:9-10).

Hate will grow in the world toward people of faith. Christians will be persecuted more and more as the Word of God is attacked and seen as an obstacle to the new laws of the land. The subpoena against us, the pastors in Houston, by Mayor Annise Parker and the lack of objection by most members of the City Council shows how little respect for the church remains in this nation, where prayer was once allowed in schools. As we testified in the courthouse during the legal fight for the right of the people to vote as the signatures turned in had requested, we gave the testimony in front of those who demanded our sermons and saw the Spirit of God in that courthouse as described in Mark 13:9-13. Hate of absolute truth is real today in America and Janet Folder in her book *The Criminalization of Christianity* exposes the reality of what is happening, "Today, expressing an absolute truth is considered *intolerance*. For fear that those who disagree might be offended, those who actually believe something are increasingly silenced."[2]

---

[2] Janet L. Folger, The Criminalization of Christianity (Oregon, Multnomah Publishers Sisters, 2005), 34.

Jesus often offended those who heard him speak about the condition of their hearts, whom he called hypocrites. *"Woe unto you, scribes and Pharisees, hypocrites! For ye are like unto whited sepulchers, which indeed appear beautiful outward, but are within full of dead men's bones, and of all uncleanness. Even so ye also outwardly appear righteous unto men, but within ye are full of hypocrisy and iniquity"* (Matthew 23:27-28).

They wanted to silence the voice that did not tolerate their way of living. This made them persecute him unto death. It is important to understand that what we tolerate today will be the norm of the society of tomorrow. Christ's crucifixion was the demonstration of hate motivated by the offended rulers and leaders of his time. Death by crucifixion was a way to shame the person being hanged. Hate is a feeling that penetrates the inner being of the offended and gives rise to aggressive and impulsive behavior.

We Love and Pray For Our Enemies

No other religion in the world teaches its followers to love their enemies as Christ Jesus commanded us to do. As a matter of fact, those who accuse us of having hate in our heart against anyone, have no understanding of what Christianity is. Otherwise, they would know that we believe the fruit of a relationship with Jesus is to express love to everyone, regardless of who they are or what they may have done. In the Gospel of Luke we read, *"But I say unto you which hear, Love your enemies, do good to them which hate you, Bless them that curse you, and pray for them which despitefully use you"* (Luke 6:27-28).

The act of praying and loving our enemies reveals the maturity of our relationship with God. In the natural, it is virtually impossible to love someone who has persecuted you, attacked you, and tried to silence your voice. However, as ministers and people of faith we know that ours isn't a battle against flesh and blood. It's spiritual warfare, which the Apostle Paul described in Ephesians 6:12. While Christians around the world are facing persecution and being killed in painful and inhumane ways by radical terrorists in the name of their gods, we Christians serve the one true God and father of our Lord Jesus Christ, who through the example of his Son on the cross, taught us to confront hate with love.

> *"Then said Jesus, Father, forgive them; for they know not what they do. And they parted his raiment, and cast lots. And the people stood*

> *beholding. And the rulers also with them derided him, saying, He saved others; let him save himself, if he be Christ, the chosen of God. And the soldiers also mocked him, coming to him, and offering him vinegar, And saying, If thou be the king of the Jews, save thyself"* (Luke 23:34-37).

Forgiveness is releasing all of the accumulated offenses, all of the attacks and insults that were aimed at us. It is to release them out of your soul and not allow anger, resentment, revengeful thoughts to take root in our spirits. Through forgiveness, we destroy the power of division, hate, and rejection.

While nailed to his cross, Jesus suffered persecution, pain, and ridicule as he gave his life a sacrifice for his enemies. Love is not equal to hate. We love and pray for our enemies as he taught us with the hope that one day they will turn from their deceptive ways. They may hate us, or believe wrongly, that we hate them. However, the reason that we stand up is our deep love for our God, our nation, our families. We pray to see our children grow up in safe environments, and to rescue some who are trapped in mental depravity. If there is to be a light in the spiritual darkness that surrounds us, it must be the light of Christ through the church, which is the only light that can regenerate, transform, and restore lives.

Hate In America

As I write this chapter, there is much hatred in America developing and being propagated by those who have lost the love and unity that makes us all Americans. Hate does the following.

1. Hate calls for vengeance of an eye for an eye, and brings about more violence. (Romans 12:19)
2. It builds walls of division instead of bridges of communication and understanding. (Ephesians 2:14)
3. Hate hardens people's hearts. (Romans 2:5)
4. Hate blinds the mind and feeds it with evil thoughts. (James 2:4)

America must return to God. Only he can heal our land and forgive our sins.

During our confrontation with the city of Houston, a few local ministers sadly remained silent and did not speak on behalf of the biblical and moral values that the church has been raised to preach and teach to its people. Some were too afraid, as pastors of mega Churches, to lose numbers of visitors and members of their congregation if they were to speak out against this immoral law that was being pushed to allow men in women's bathrooms. Their defense for not engaging was that we are first to pray, and then to love everyone. However, they must not have read the scriptures where Jesus confronted the wicked rulers of his time.

Even the familiar revival scripture, 2 Chronicles 7:14, teaches us to humble ourselves and confess the sins of the land. We can pray and confess within the walls of our churches, but the church must come out of the walls into the streets, into City Hall, into the bridges and highways of the city, and raise a voice that calls for justice and biblical truth. That is real love and it has nothing to do with hatred. Jesus did not oppose the Pharisees and rulers because he hated them, but because only the truth could set them free. (John 8:32)

Jesus told them the truth in love.

1. He told them that they did the lusts of their father the devil. (John 8:44)
2. He warned them that the Father would one day tell them to depart from him, for they were workers of iniquity. (Luke 13:27)
3. Jesus called King Herod a fox. (Luke 13:32)
4. Jesus overthrew the money-changer's tables, and called them thieves in God's house. (John 2:15)

Hatred Toward God's Word

One of the greatest abominations of our times happened on Friday, June 26, 2015 when the Supreme Court of the United States ruled that marriage was no longer defined as just the union between a man and a woman. Marriage had been stolen from the one who created it, God himself. It had been modified, redefined to justify the depravity of man. It was a five to four decision that immediately produced celebrations all over the nation claiming that love always wins. The Supreme Court's decision was not love winning, but hate toward God's Word that prevailed in the courthouse.

> *"Woe unto them that are wise in their own eyes, And prudent in their own sight! Woe unto them that are mighty to drink wine, and men of strength to mingle strong drink: Which justify the wicked for reward, and take away the righteousness of the righteous from him"* (Isaiah 5:21-23)!

The wine of the cup of perversion and abomination had been drunk by the highest court of the land and they considered themselves wise in their own eyes. They ignored the truth that marriage is a God-union between a man and a woman only, and clearly confirmed by the words of Jesus himself, when he said, *"For this cause shall a man leave his father and mother, and cleave to his wife; and they twain shall be one flesh: so then they are no more twain, but one flesh"* (Mark 10:7-8).

The only love that wins is the love that is grounded biblical truth, love that respects the laws of creation. The fruit of love in marriage comes out of a relationship based on the original intention, design, and purpose of God. That is why God designed the man's body to have a relationship with his wife, and as a result of that love be able to reproduce. The covenant of marriage is to be a parallel of the love that God has for the church and how he has promised to respect and honor her.

> *"So ought men to love their wives as their own bodies. He that loveth his wife loveth himself. For no man ever yet hated his own flesh; but nourisheth and cherisheth it, even as the Lord the church"* (Ephesians 5:28-29).

Love of a man toward his wife is a measuring tool of how much that man loves himself. Hate does not exist where love lives. This is why, the greatest commandment is to love God first and then our neighbor;

> *"Master, which is the great commandment in the law? Jesus said unto him, Thou shalt love the Lord thy God with all thy heart, and with*

all thy soul, and with all thy mind. This is the first and great commandment. And the second is like unto it, Thou shalt love thy neighbor as thyself" (Matthew 22:36-39).

To disobey these commandments is to hate God, hate his Word, and to not know what love is.

Chapter 4:
Stand

There are times for us to stand and not sit complacently while the values of our land are being stolen. It takes courage, dignity, love, and determination to stand when many are shrinking in fear, ignoring the disintegration of the once respected and untouchable moral values of the country. Standing is more than a thought. It's more than a desire to do something. It is to take action.

In the Bible there is a powerful story of a man named Shammah who stood in the midst of a field that the enemy had come to destroy. The word *Shammah* in Hebrew means obedient, and it is obedience to God and his Word that enables us to stand and defend our religious liberty that's being assaulted by injustice and immorality.

> *"And after him was Shammah the son of Agee the Hararite. And the Philistines were gathered together into a troop, where was a piece of ground full of lentils: and the people fled from the Philistines. But he stood in the midst of the ground, and defended it, and slew the*

Philistines: and the LORD *wrought a great victory"* (2 Samuel 23:11-12).

The ground was full of lentils (a food crop that produces a round, flat seed, like a pea). Shammah defended those lentils until God gave him the victory. Today, more than ever, there is a call to every pastor, to every Christian, to every father and mother, to every believer in America to stand and protect the lentils. The lentils are the principles that compose society and define marriage, family, morality, and justice. These principles grew on the foundation of God's Word.

Fear Will Make You Remain Seated

Fear will cause one to sit quietly for fear to speak, and fear to reject the worldly views of liberalism. It is to deny our heritage as Americans, and most importantly as Bible believing children of the Most High God. A transformation will not come until someone stands for what is right. The voice of equality that suppresses the voice of one nation under God can only prevail if we allow it to be louder than our own.

The scriptures teach us that during the trial of Jesus there were two voices. One voice said, "Crucify him;" and the other voice sought to protect him.

> *"Pilate therefore, willing to release Jesus, spake again to them. But they cried, saying, crucify him, crucify him. And he said unto them the third time, Why, what evil hath he done? I have found no cause of death in him: I will therefore chastise him, and let him go. And they were instant with loud voices, requiring that he might be crucified. And the voices of them and of the chief priests prevailed"* (Luke 23:20-23).

It was at that time that the Apostle Peter watched from a distance, standing with the others trying to warm himself, because it was cold. He denied knowing Jesus three times. Peter wanted nothing to do with the trial, nothing to do with Jesus, he was completely dominated by his fear. It kept him restricted from expressing his real thoughts and position. To be standing like Peter was, and not speak, is as tragic as to be sitting. It is cold in America, many are just spectators of the news, spectators of the attacks on religious liberty, who have yet to realize that time is running out.

> *"Then saith the damsel that kept the door unto Peter, Art not thou also one of this man's disciples? He saith, I am not. And the servants and officers stood there, who had made a fire of coals; for it was cold: and they warmed*

> *themselves: and Peter stood with them, and warmed himself"* (John 18:17-18).

Prophecy is being fulfilled, the end times are unfolding, and Christians will have to make a decision as they are going to be confronted more and more by those who recognize them. If you are a man or a woman of faith, of family principles and believe in the Creator, then you will be approached and interrogated. Peter had this experience and he was not ready to stand, as a result, he denied it all with great emotion until he heard the cock crow as Jesus had told him he would, in Mark 14:72.

> *"And Simon Peter stood and warmed himself. They said therefore unto him, Art not thou also one of his disciples? He denied it, and said, I am not. One of the servants of the high priest, being his kinsman whose ear Peter cut off, saith, did not I see thee in the garden with him? Peter then denied again: and immediately the cock crew"* (John 18:25-27).

Fear is the lack of perfect in love, and it will bring torment to anyone that submits to it.

> *"There is no fear in love; but perfect love casteth out fear: because fear hath torment. He that feareth is not made perfect in love"* (1 John 4:18).

When people of various colors, ethnicities, and backgrounds stand together to defend justice, and to protect their families, no abusive governmental power, local or national, will be able to overcome them. Peter learned that standing without a voice was as bad as to remain seated.

Fifty days later, Peter defeated his fear, after the death and resurrection of Jesus Christ. While he and 120 others were in the upper room there came a fire and authority from heaven upon all that were gathered in that place. The power to stand and spiritual marching orders were given to them. Immediately Peter stood up in their midst and declared the truth without reservation. *"But Peter, standing up with the eleven, lifted up his voice, and said unto them, Ye men of Judaea, and all ye that dwell at Jerusalem, be this known unto you, and hearken to my words"* (Acts 2:14).

It was the beginning of a revival, an uprising of a people united by the convictions of their hearts, knowing that God was in control. Notice, that it was not only Peter. Eleven were standing with him. Three thousand accepted his words and believed, according to Acts 3:19.

The Church Has a Voice

The church was not born weak in the Book of Acts. It was born with power and authority. It was born with a voice that boldly spoke, despite being persecuted. The church is the hope of America as it holds the truth of creation, the dignity of morality, and the justice of Creator God. The church is not a building. It is the body of Christ made up of believers who have been forgiven and cleansed by the blood of the Jesus.

The voice of the church is what the founders of our nation heard and respected, it is a voice that was always heard by those in government and in any position of authority. This is why there is a resistance to the voice of the church, a resistance that comes from those who want to do their own will and set themselves as equal to God.

1. They want to silence the voice of the church—of freedom of religion.
2. They want to intimidate the cry for moral and biblical values.
3. They want to crucify the church and kill the faith of Americans.

4. They will challenge your heart-based beliefs, and if necessary, will imprison you for not allowing them to redefine your faith.
5. A church without a voice is a church without a pastor.
6. A pastor without a church is a pastor with no voice.
7. Freedom without religion is the burial of the inner man.
8. Religion without freedom is slavery of the inner man.

Every Pastor Must Stand

This is why the pastors of every church, large and small, suburban and inner-city, every leader of a flock must stand and lead. Pastors must not only stand behind the pulpit during their regular services to preach, but they must also take their stand on the battlefield. A pastor standing behind the pulpit of a church building can only address his congregation, but a pastor who stands on the battlefield, defending the faith and moral biblical values, speaks to the nation. The battlefield includes every street corner, every community, every town, city and state in the nation. Stand with the fearful and you will be intimidated. But, stand with the brave and you will be strengthened. To stand, pastors must know that with whom, how, when, why, and where they stand makes a difference.

1. With whom you stand reveals your integrity.
2. How you stand reveals your character.
3. When you stand reveals your discernment.
4. Why you stand reveals your convictions.
5. Where you stand reveals your wisdom.

Every Pastor Must Speak

The words of a pastor must be those that reflect the profound truth of God's Word without compromise. A pastor must remember that silence is not leadership, but a pastor must follow the description of the good shepherd as taught by Jesus.

> *"Verily, verily, I say unto you, He that entereth not by the door into the sheepfold, but climbeth up some other way, the same is a thief and a robber. But he that entereth in by the door is the shepherd of the sheep. To him the porter openeth; and the sheep hear his voice: and he calleth his own sheep by name, and leadeth them out. And when he putteth forth his own*

> *sheep, he goeth before them, and the sheep follow him: for they know his voice"* (John 10:1-4).

Every congregation of believers must know the voice of their pastor and every pastor must do the following,

1. Enter by the door. He must identify himself with the people as their pastor.
2. His voice must be heard. When a pastor does not speak out, other voices will take his place and mislead the people.
3. He leads them out. Pastors show the people how to come out of deception and ignorance.
4. He goes before them. Pastors serve through the example of their own actions and words.
5. Gives his life for them. His ministry is to invest in others.
6. Pastors never flee. Pastors stand and face corruption and deception, calling everything by its name without fear.

In the beginning, God spoke light into existence, and separated it from darkness. When a pastor speaks truth, there is a separation of right and wrong. Pastors should speak God's unnegotiable truth. *Truth* is not for sale. To put a price on *truth* is to believe the lie of equal rights. It forces one to surrender their faith to the choices of others. A pastor does not speak for or to himself. He speaks for the God who called him, so all may hear. (John 17)

How a pastor speaks, reveals his soul (his mind, will, and emotions).

What a pastor speaks, reveals his heart (his spirit and inner man).

His words can carry the power of truth to ignite a fire of revival, just as they can carry the deception of a lie to extinguish the fire of truth. To fail to speak while observing injustice is to speak silently in favor of it.

The Power of the Vote

The City of Houston was denying its people their greatest right—their right to vote. When the voice of the people is not heard, then government has become the abuser of the people rather than the servant of the people who elected it. A vote expresses the citizens' choice. It is a powerful voice that impacts the future generations. The church and people with moral values must become involved in every election and use the power of their votes. As a Latino pastor I believe that the sleeping giant, America's Hispanic vote, is about to wake up in America and let its voice be heard like never before.

Currently, as the Director of the Hispanic Church Development in the *Texas Pastor Council*, we are working to train Hispanic leaders. As I travel around and teach on biblical issues, I constantly find motivated pastors who are rising up and working in unity.

Each of us is responsible to vote. We must never allow anything or anyone to stop us from exercising that God-given right. For us to fail to vote, is to allow others to make decisions for us; the result of which may be harmful. To be informed and well-prepared will always bring a voter the satisfaction of having made the best choice in any given election. Every Christian should have a plan of action, a strategy and a clear vision of how to get involved in their communities.

Jesus knew his purpose for coming into the world. He said, *"He that committeth sin is of the devil; for the devil sinneth from the beginning. For this purpose the Son of God was manifested, that he might destroy the works of the devil"* (1 John 3:8).

One's vote can support sin or oppose it. A vote for the right candidate will cause the people to rejoice. A vote for the wrong candidate will provoke them to mourn.

"When the righteous are in authority, the people rejoice: But when the wicked beareth rule, the people mourn" (Proverbs 29:2).

Chapter 5:
In Conclusion

There is an attack on America's pulpits today. It will worsen as evil advances its agenda to destroy the right of the people's free practice of religion. Time is running out for the church in America. Only a genuine revival at the altars of the church will cause a wave of godly people to fill our cities with the transforming truth that restores the hearts of men.

It all begins with heartfelt repentance as we ask God to forgive and cleanse ourselves and our nation of the abominations that are being done in the land. Entire cities have turned away from morality, and invited all kinds of immorality into their streets while celebrating their uncleanness with pride parades. *"But chiefly them that walk after the flesh in the lust of uncleanness, and despise government. Presumptuous are they, self-willed, they are not afraid to speak evil of dignities"* (2 Peter 2:10).

The City of Houston demanded the sermons of pastors as a direct threat that they either stop preaching righteousness and truth, or be brought into court. Money has become the argument for promoting sin in the name of equality as major businesses are always threatening to move out and bring economic sanctions to our cities. We need the Elijah kind of leadership today that will not give up until the fire falls upon the rebuilt altars.

> *"And it came to pass at the time of the offering of the evening sacrifice, that Elijah the prophet came near, and said, LORD God of Abraham, Isaac, and of Israel, let it be known this day that thou art God in Israel, and that I am thy servant, and that I have done all these things at thy word. Hear me, O LORD, hear me, that this people may know that thou art the LORD God, and that thou hast turned their heart back again. Then the fire of the LORD fell, and consumed the burnt sacrifice, and the wood, and the stones, and the dust, and licked up the water that was in the trench. And when all the people saw it, they fell on their faces: and they said, The LORD, he is the God; the LORD, he is the God"* (1 Kings 18:36-39).

We must come to the altar of God and pray that God will turn the hearts of men to seek his face. Holy fire must return to the church and continue to burn until God's people fall on their faces and recognize that the

Lord is God. The preaching of God's full Word must return to our pulpits. The passion that Paul speaks about must be the same passion today among the leaders of the church. *"For I have not shunned to declare unto you all the counsel of God"* (Acts 20:27).

The Apostle Paul declared the full counsel of God. He understood that the complete message must be given without fragmentation. One problem today is that Christians are allowing the deterioration of justice, and corruption is spreading to all levels of government. It's exemplified by pastors of mega-churches who are afraid to preach the entire counsel of God for fear of decreasing their membership attendance. They excuse themselves by claiming that their ministry assignment is to "only preach the love of God," and nothing else. To allow society to sink deeper and deeper in sin and not declare the truth isn't love. Love warns people of the dangers of their choices.

The Bible is not being opened anymore at many pulpits. Many pastors are composing their messages to sound appealing to the human ear and to entertain the people while they are at church. This causes a generation of Christians who have no understanding of the Bible, right and wrong, and their responsibilities as Christians.

> *"Therefore my people are gone into captivity, because they have no knowledge: and their honorable men are famished, and their multitude dried up with thirst"* (Isaiah 5:13).

When we who are called into ministry become men-pleasers instead of God-followers, we end up with a society that has no discernment of good and evil.

> *"For do I now persuade men, or God? Or do I seek to please men? For if I yet pleased men, I should not be the servant of Christ"* (Galatians 1:10).

We need servants of God today who will answer the Most High calling of preaching the gospel, and of being light in a world invaded by darkness. God give us men and women who will stand and not sit down; who will speak and not be silent; and who will do what needs to be done without fear.

As one of the five Houston pastors who were served the subpoena for my sermons, I pray and believe with all my heart that that there is still hope for our country. That hope is in the Lord Jesus Christ, through his church, which he paid for with his own blood. The church must arise and remember that when it stands and declares the truth, the gates of hell will not prevail against it.

"And I say also unto thee, 'That thou art Peter, and upon this rock I will build my church; and the gates of hell shall not prevail against it'" (Matthew 16:18).

Appendix A

Request Number 12 of The Subpoena for Pastors' Sermons

In order to reduce the issues that will need to be decided by the court, however, Defendants revise Request No. 12.

Request No. 12 originally read:

All speeches, presentations, or sermons related to HERO, the Petition, Mayor Annise Parker, homosexuals, or gender identity prepared by, delivered by, revised by, or approved by you or in your possession.

Defendants hereby revise Request No. 12 as follows:

All speeches or presentations related to HERO or the Petition prepared by, delivered by, revised by, or approved by you or in your possession.

Conclusion

Defendants' Preliminary Response will be supplemented to address the remaining issues raised in the Motion and Memorandum filed by the subpoena recipients. For the reasons set forth herein, and for other reasons to be provided in a supplement to this preliminary response, Defendants ask that the Court overrule any objection to Request No. 12, as revised.

Respectfully submitted,

By: /s/ *David Feldman*

CITY OF HOUSTON LEGAL DEPARTMENT

Appendix B - Pictures

For weeks we spent full days at the courthouse, praying and letting the judge know how important the right to vote is for the people of Houston.

Pastors united as one in the fight for religious freedom.

We stood as a coalition of pastors representing all colors, minorities, and backgrounds. This is the church standing for moral and biblical values.

I'm standing next to one of God's generals, Pastor F.N. Williams, Sr.
Pastor Williams is a man respected for his leadership and love for truth.
He is pastor of Antioch Missionary Baptist Church.

This is one of the flyers (in Spanish) that was used to invite people
in front of City Hall to demand the people's right to vote.

Pastor Hernan addresses the Texas Pastors Council at a quarterly strategy meeting.

My wife Wendy and I, standing next to Pastors Steve and Becky Riggle.

Texas Senator Ted Cruz came to stand with us when he heard that we pastors had received the subpoena for our sermons. My wife Wendy (at the left) and I are grateful to Senator Cruz for his courageous leadership in defense of the Constitution of the United States of America.

Our great Governor of Texas, Gregg Abbott, celebrates with Wendy and I the signing of a law to protect Texas' pastors and their religious liberty. Governor Abbott immediately sent Mayor Parker a letter objecting to her actions to subpoena the pastors in Houston.

Pastor David Welch, USPC Director, a true warrior and general,
led the pastors in unity to stand for righteousness and truth against the
lies of immorality and injustice. We all are blessed to be under his guidance.

Attorney Andy Taylor

Max A. Miller

Pastor Willie Davis

Pastors standing for truth.

www.ingramcontent.com/pod-product-compliance
Lightning Source LLC
Chambersburg PA
CBHW070121080526
44586CB00013B/1347